Contents

Shelter is a need

Living things need shelter.

A shelter is a home.

It is a place to live and grow.

Shelters help to keep living things warm. They help to keep living things safe.

Types of shelters

People build houses.
A house has walls and a
roof. Houses protect people
from bad weather.

A polar bear digs
in the snow.
She makes a den.
Her cubs are safe
and warm in the den.

An owl finds a shelter in a hole in a tree. It is a good place to rest and stay dry.

13

Can you see this nest in the tree? The bird made it for her eggs. They are safe and warm. When the eggs hatch, the baby birds will live in the nest.

15

A world of homes

Some animals live in warm places. Some live in cold places. Different animals need different homes.

Some animals carry their own homes!

A turtle carries its hard shell.

The shell is its home.

It protects the turtle.

Some animals find shelters in nature. Others make their own shelters.

What shelter homes can you name?

Glossary

cub a young mammal such as a cheetah, bear or lion

den a place where a wild animal may live; a den may be a hole in the ground or the trunk of a tree

grow to get bigger in size

need to require something; you need food, shelter and air to stay alive

shelter a place where a living thing can stay safe and live

weather the daily state of air outdoors in a certain place; weather changes with each season

Find out more

A Place to Live (Wants Versus Needs), Linda Staniford (Raintree, 2015)

All About Forests (Habitats), Christine Mia Gardeski (Raintree, 2018)

What Do Living Things Need? Elizabeth Austen (Teacher Created Materials, 2015)

Websites

Habitats and the environment
www.bbc.co.uk/bitesize/topics/zx882hv

What do animals need to survive?
www.bbc.co.uk/bitesize/topics/z6882hv/articles/zx38wmn

Comprehension questions

1. Why do living things need shelter?

2. What types of homes do animals make?

3. What can a shelter protect living things from?

Index